NORTHUMBERLAND
SCHOOLS LIBRARY SERVICE

GEORGE

Family World

My Mum

Caryn Jenner

W
FRANKLIN WATTS
LONDON • SYDNEY

Sharing this book

This book shows the variety of roles that a mother plays in children's lives around the world. It provides a useful starting point to discuss how families everywhere are similar, but that each child's family is different and special.

• Remember that families are formed in different ways and a mother can be a step-mother, an adoptive mother, a foster mother or anyone else that the child thinks of as a mother.

• Being a mum is a rewarding job, but sometimes it can be difficult. Ask your GP, health visitor or school for advice.

These organisations also offer help to families:
Family Lives – www.familylives.org.uk, Parentline 0808 800 2222
Family Links – www.familylinks.org.uk
Gingerbread (especially for single-parent families) – www.gingerbread.org.uk

First published in 2013 by Franklin Watts
Copyright © Franklin Watts 2013

Franklin Watts
338 Euston Road
London NW1 3BH

Franklin Watts Australia
Level 17/207 Kent Street
Sydney, NSW 2000

All rights reserved.

Series Editor: Sarah Peutrill
Series Designer: Ruth Walton

Dewey number: 306.8'743
ISBN: 978 1 4451 1928 1
Printed in Malaysia

Franklin Watts is a division of Hachette Children's Books, an Hachette UK company. www.hachette.co.uk

Please note:
Some of the pictures in this book are posed by models. All scenarios are fictitious and any similarities to people, living or dead, are purely coincidental.

Picture credits: uri Acurs/istockphoto: 23tl. antigoniigoni/istockphoto: 6r. Argus/ Shutterstock: 14b. Maria Bell/ Shutterstock: 6tl. c/Shutterstock: 5c. Augusto Cabral/ Shutterstock: 9ct, 12cl. Cobalt 88/Shutterstock: 16cb. digitalskillet/istockphoto: front cover, 6cl. Duncan 1890/ istockphoto: 23tc. erdem/Shutterstock: 4t. gabor2100/ Shutterstock: 20-21. Xavier Gallego/istockphoto: 23b. Globe Turner/Shutterstock: 12b, 16cr, 19t. adam golabek/ Shutterstock: 8t. granata1111/Shutterstock: 9t. Bartosz Hadyniak/istockphoto: back cover, 4c. hadynyah/ istockphoto: 18c. iofoto/ istockphoto: 9tb. Jessmine/ Shutterstock: 12cr. michaeljung/Shutterstock: 18ba. kali9/ istockphoto: 7c. Alekesy Klints/Shutterstock: 13t, 15ca, 18b. Morgan Lane Photography/Shutterstock: 16c. Artem Loskutnikov/Shutterstock: 7t. Nolte Lourens/Shutterstock: 11c. Steve Luker/ istockphoto: 23tcl. Geo Martinez/istockphoto: 23cl. MIXA/Alamy: 13c. naphtalina/istockphoto: 23tr. Martin Novak/Shutterstock: 19c. Patrick Foto /Shutterstock: 17c, 22. Thomas M Perkins/Shutterstock: 10c. pink cotton candy/istockphoto: 23cr. Pixel Memoirs/Shutterstock: 15tb. Denis & Yulia Pogostins/Shutterstock: 14c. Alexander Raths/Shutterstock: 5t. rehoboth foto/Shutterstock: 10t, 17t. robodread /Shutterstock: 11b. Ken Seet/Alamy: 16b. shaunl/istockphoto: 9c. Taipan Kid/Shutterstock: 18t. Anatoly Tiplyashin/Shutterstock: 15t. vitapix/istockphoto: 12tl. Catherine Yeulet/istockphoto: 8c. Zurijeta/Shutterstock: 15c. Every attempt has been made to clear copyright. Should there be any inadvertent omission please apply to the publisher for rectification.

Contents

This is my mum

Think about your mum and the things she does to care for you. All over the world, mothers love their children and look after them.

Elisa's family is from Bolivia. Elisa calls her mum 'Mami' or 'Madre'.

Luke lives in Great Britain. When his mum adopted him, they became a family. He calls her 'Mummy'.

What do you call your mother?

My mum loves me

Mothers show love for their children in many ways.

At their home in Mexico, Carolina's mum gives her a kiss to show that she loves her.

Theo and his mum live in Cyprus. When he is sad, his mum cuddles him to make him feel better.

In Ecuador, Sofia's mum tries to teach her good behaviour. But she loves Sofia no matter what.

How does your mum show that she loves you?

Looking after me

Mothers try to keep their children safe, clean and healthy. They make sure their children eat, sleep and learn.

In China, Chen's mum makes sure he has healthy food to eat, like yummy noodles with vegetables.

Maria lives with her dad and step-mum in Spain. When Maria grazes her knee, her step-mum puts a plaster on it.

Many children in Canada go to school on a bus. Sarah's mum takes her to the bus stop every morning.

Mums often need help. Does someone help to look after you? Who?

Helping me

Children often need help from their mothers while they learn to do new things.

Jasmine's family lives in the United States. Her mum helps Jasmine to sound out words when they read together. Her little sister, Mei, tries to read too.

In Uganda, Samuel's mum helps him to tie his shoelaces. She says soon Samuel will learn to do it himself.

Playing together

Playing together is fun! Mothers and children can simply enjoy being together.

At home in Italy, Marco and his mum build an amazing house with bricks.

In Denmark, Katrin and her sister, Freja, have two mothers. Together they explore the countryside.

Ken's family lives in Japan. He loves going to the park with his mum. She helps Ken on the climbing frame.

?

What do you and your mum play together? Ask your mum what she likes to play.

Being busy

Mothers are often busy working and doing chores. Sometimes children can help.

Marta and her mum are busy in the garden at their home in Poland. Marta feels proud of her hard work.

Liam visits his dad and step-mum in Ireland. He washes the dishes while his step-mum waits to dry them.

In Egypt, Ahmed's mum shows him how she does her work on the computer.

Working together can be fun, but sometimes you need to keep yourself busy while your mum gets on with the work.

Special times

Birthdays, holidays and other special times give mothers and children a chance to celebrate and do special things together.

In South Africa, Nicole's mum makes her birthday into an extra-special celebration.

During the festival of Diwali in India, Priya and her brother Adil light candles with their mum.

Farah and her mum go on holiday to the seaside in Malaysia. They have fun building sandcastles.

What are the special times you enjoy with your mum?

Mum makes me feel special

All over the world, mothers make their children feel special.

Rashmi's family lives in Sri Lanka. Rashmi likes it when her mum makes her laugh. They laugh a lot!

Michael and his mum live in Jamaica. He feels good when his mum says she is proud of him.

In Australia, Chloe and her mum have a great big cuddle.

?

How does your mum make you feel special? How do you make her feel special?

A world of families

Children just like you live all around the world. Every child's family is different and special in its own way, and every mother is different and special in her own way. But families everywhere also have many things in common.

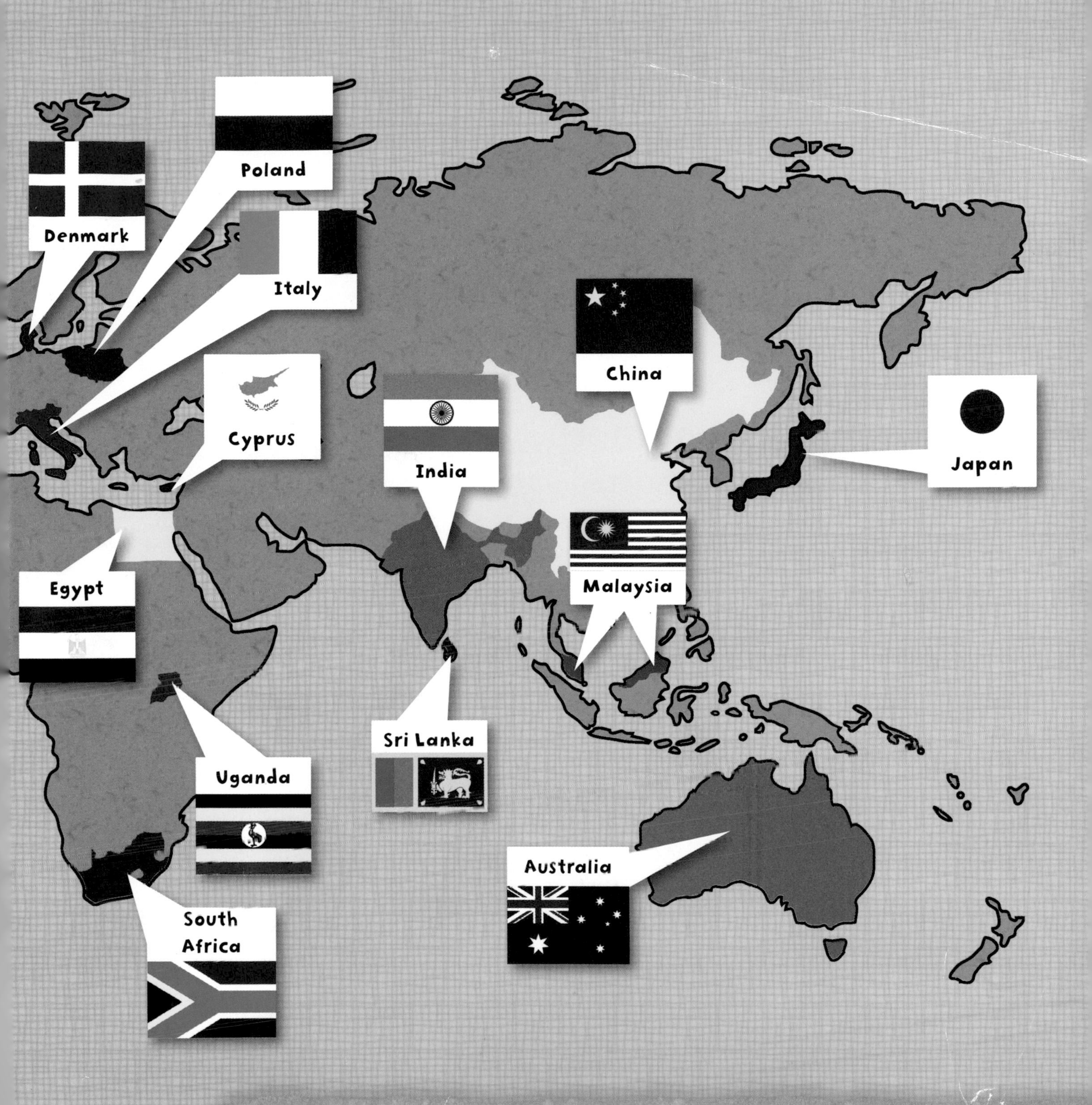

The families in this book live in the countries marked on this map. Can you find the flag that goes with each family in the book?

Activities

Tell your mum why she's special

Make an award certificate for her. Write 'I think you're special because...' or 'You're brilliant because...' and list the things she does that you think are special.

Find out how children around the world say 'mother'.

Find out how to say mother in different languages. Ask friends who speak other languages, or look it up in books or on the Internet. Here are a few languages to get you started:

Spanish – Madre
French – Mère
German – Mutter
Somali – Hoya
Punjabi – Mai
Japanese – Okaasan

Pretend to be a mum

Play a dressing-up game. Pretend you are a mum while your mum pretends she is a child. Pretend to do the things that she usually does for you, such as comforting her if she gets hurt or tucking her in bed. You can get ideas from this book.

Make a family tree

A family tree shows the people in your family. Draw a picture of yourself and each person in your family, or use photos. On another sheet of paper, draw a tree. Stick your family pictures onto your tree. Your family tree can show the people you live with, or it can show lots of people in your family. You can even include your pets!

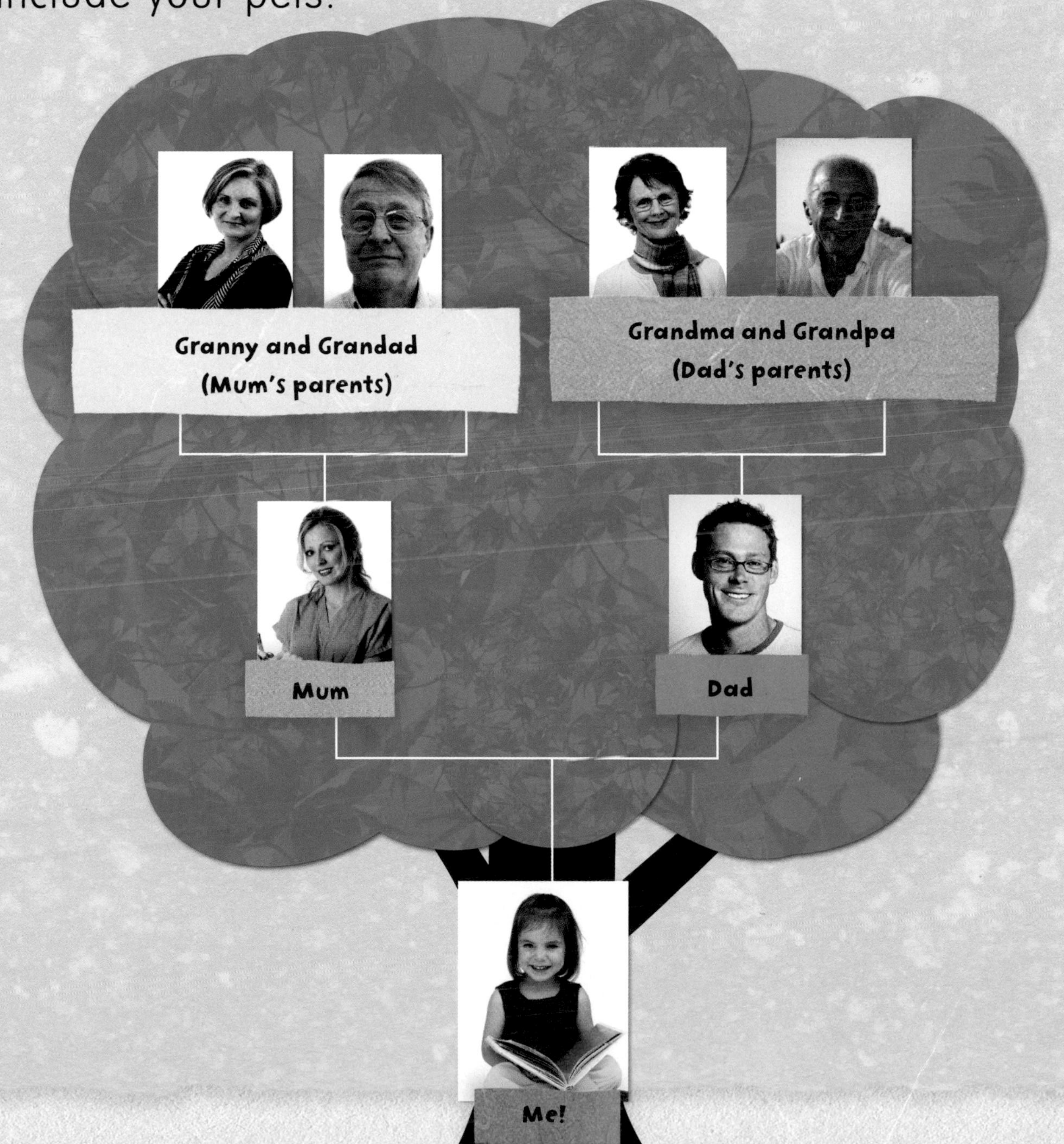

Words about families

Here are some words you may use when talking about families.

Adopted – becoming part of a family that is not the family you were born into

Divorced – when parents split up and are no longer married

Family – a group of people who love and care for each other and are usually related

Foster mum or dad – grown-ups who look after you in their family if your parents can't

Grandparents – your mum and dad's parents

Half-brother or half-sister – a brother or sister who has the same mum or dad as you, but the other parent is different

Parents – your mum and dad

Siblings – brothers and sisters

Step-brother or step-sister – the son or daughter of your step-mum or step-dad

Step-mum or step-dad – if your parents are divorced and one of them marries again, the new wife or husband would be your step-mum or step-dad

Index